Bug Bites And Their Scars

They Do Not Define You

Stephanie Pomper

BookLeaf Publishing

India | USA | UK

Made with ❤ on the BookLeaf Publishing Platform

www.bookleafpub.in

www.bookleafpub.com

Dedication

to little me. to little you.

we are deserving of love.

Preface

there comes a moment in time where you just don't care anymore. it all becomes meaningless. words are just words and your oxygen is more precious to your own lungs than to others ears. things you gave away without a second thought become things you keep to yourself. the weight of it all becomes too much to carry, so you simply put it down. not to say you no longer feel those things, but more so that you've accepted that things cannot and will not change. you embrace the concept of endings and appreciate the good days, until the bad days exceed them. that is when you can look back on them fondly with a smile, and release the weight of what's been occupying your mind for months. at first it will sting, as any simple insect bite does. it is important to recognize the insignificance of that bug on your overall life, and notice how quickly that sting will pass if you simply allow it. breathe in, and breathe out. take back the oxygen that has always been your birth right, create new mechanisms to be utilized in feature experiences, and learn to love yourself as yourself again, and nobody else's.

it is also important to recognize that sometimes it takes multiple bites before you accept you're truly being bitten. there is no fault in discovering this, despite having healed scars. the fact of the matter is there is bravery in recognition of the pain endured. i hope you understand that your value did not diminish during this passage.

over time wounds can grow. however, over time wounds will also heal, *if you allow them.*

i'm not asking you to solve it all at once. i'm not even asking you to eat a full meal.

start by feeding your lungs, and just *breathe.*

Acknowledgements

1. remaining residuals

i'm too young to have a mid-life crisis

my therapist recommended i start by identifying things
that are part of who i am
my name
my age
my address
my occupation
my siblings
my education

we broadened my search by identifying things that i
enjoy
objects
things
tv shows
foods
activities
hobbies

i'm still confused

everything listed is associated with someone else
i can tell you where every object came from
my things are a collection of my adventures
tv shows are linked to the era i watched them
foods are a limitation of what i think i'm worth
activities are thought of but never performed
hobbies are collectibles awaiting me on my shelves

where do they end and i begin

2. seaking solitude

i'm not sure if someone with an internal dialogue is ever
truly alone

i replay it all, down to every small detail

words misplaced by anger
punching created from rage
actions fueled by resentment
fishing spawned from mistrust
tears shed by sadness
longing born from love

i reran the tape today
and i know i will tomorrow
until the static overtakes the track
at some point i will understand it was not something i
did

i am not a reflection of you

3. meaningful minutes

i'm not sure what 9 minutes has ever meant to anyone

i used to set my subsequent alarms 4 minutes apart
so they wouldn't go off at the same time
that way if i did accidentally fall asleep
the reawake period would be soon enough
for me to not fall into a deep slumber again

i was falling in a different way

one day you were there when i awoke
i would watch your chest rise and fall
count the lashes brimming your eyelids
admire your nose and cheekbones
wish away the bags under your eyes

i stopped needing the 4 minute alarms

trace the edges of your skin
memorize the corners of your lips
gasp as you pulled me in closer
bury my head in your collar bone
whisper i love you one last time

i started to love waking up to you

the alarm is echoing in the emptiness
my arm naturally reaches for your head
instead of bedhead i find an empty pillow
its pitch black in my room still
i must've only snoozed once

i bought black out curtains for you

i jolt up in a haze of confusion
throw on the first outfit i can find
i'm already late before i've left home
i don't understand where the time goes
where it went then, or where it goes now

*hitting snooze on an iPhone is supposed to give you 9
minutes*

4. desirable dysphonia

there are methods used to create music

a flip of a note
a quick crescendo
a sudden dissonance
a harmonized resolution

your favorites were the imperfect ones

a note that ends in a break
a squeak that shows control
a word not fully sung
a phrase left unfinished

all meant to add more feeling to the piece

my emotions are on my sleeves
my volumes changing throughout
my word choices selected so carefully
my passion evaporates from my mouth

i've never been as raw as i am right now

my quivers relay a shaky cadence
my vocal chords cave in on me
my panic attacks force my sentences short
my whimpers escaping in resentment

mine isn't desirable to you

5. generational gashes

do you want children?

i am struggling with my own mental battles
while simultaneously brushing my teeth and eating
i'm nearly 30 and don't know what i want to be when i
grow up
there are things from my youth i've not addressed yet

i know if i have children, i don't want to give them what
i had
i don't want to implant insecurities because of not
ridding myself of my own
i want them to be carefree and trusting
i hope they never question my reasoning for loving them

i want them to know
their mother loves them
their father loves them
it was never a question of value
it's okay to cry and be human
there are healthy ways to communicate
i will always be on their team

how can i instill values i don't yet embrace?

6. adverse abandonment

the first time is coincidence
the second is just bad luck
when's the third?

when i was 6 i didn't know what was happening
when i was 12 i was filled with disdain
when i was 17 i was just happy to have you back

i know it wasn't my fault
but i can't help but ponder
was it something i said
perhaps something i did
i think if you would've told me
i would have tried to fix it
sure i was only a child
but i was your child

i wanted nothing more than to be loved by you

I have developed an innate fear, a deep rooted belief
a genuine understanding that everyone will leave me
a friend
a lover
a brother

if i could get little me to understand that she was hurt
but that hurt doesn't equate to human intention
if i could get her to see that we are lovable
but that humans make regretful decisions

i think i might get through to her, in time
but for now she's distracted
watching my siblings live the life i deserved
witnessing the life stolen from me
i'm not really sure how to calm her down
i understand it more than she knows
but there's nothing to do now

you've hurt her
she hurts me

she wanted nothing more than to be loved by you

7. negligible no

i said no

what was i wearing
what time of day was it
what kind of establishment was it at
what kind of friends do i keep
what kind of drugs did i take
what was i drinking
what did i post online
what was my dating history
what kind of make-up did i have on

i stopped saying no
began saying nothing
that still isn't a yes
that's a "if he's a good person he won't"

spoiler: he does

no isn't worth losing my life over

8. benevolent bravery

absolutely
there is a bravery in wearing rose colored glasses
being able to see the light in the world
admire how it shines in the darkest of places
viewing every set back as a challenge
a building block of your character

alternatively
there is a bravery in feeling the gray clouds
embracing the mist that they bring
knowing everything in life ends
and choosing to continue living anyway
a stepping stone in your path

if we were to be able to combine these mindsets
feel the intense sorrow of a misstep
alongside with the opportunity it brings
it is a simple term in economics
surely if we try, our emotions can grow together

show me the light and i'll share my shadows

9. imaginative insecurities

i don't remember when i stopped liking my body
i don't know if i truly ever did
i do know i don't like it anymore

i hold my breathe in pictures
i angle my jaw and chin just right
i wear slightly roomy tops
not enough for attention of bagginess
but not enough to see where my body begins

it's weird think i've lost 30 lbs
where did i lose that from
why are certain shirts still tight

occasionally i'll have a day of loving my body
usually in a cute outfit and make-up
imposter syndrome
they say you have to fake it until you make it
how long of faking it does it take

please stay until it happens

10. letting loose

undo
unset alarms within silenced cell phones
i shed the fear of you seeing my bones
undressed limbs entangled in the sheets
filling the time with sweet little treats
unscheduled time free to fill however
i could lie right here with you forever
undetermined futures destined to forge
i giggle as you eat away like a gorge
unbrushed hair tangled from friction
you have become my new addiction

to redo
two bodies aligned like a glove
eskimo kisses for warming my nose
four sleepy eyes full of love
fuzzy socks for warming your toes
six tapestries all around and above
body warmth replacing our clothes
eight snacks we are both full of
as we continue watching your shows
ten tiny moments only we know whereof
as the say, so it goes

11. painful pursuits

it is a little funny when you think about it. so many
things in life have a very clear beginning: an age, a job, a
school grade, a relationship, a marriage, an adoption,
even the book you are reading now.

for so many things it is clear yet despite my turbulent
efforts, i cannot identify starting points for my growing
pains. the ways in which you've changed me, curated my
thoughts to realize everything at once while knowing
nothing at all.

the way my head is an internal merry-go-round
the way my memory forgets we were happy once
the way my eyes search for you in every item they see
the way my tears fall as if chained to a weighted anchor
dropped into a black hole
the way my throat becomes too narrow to let me even
whisper
the way my chest aches under the bricks of your words
the way my heart lingers on **_what if i stayed_**

the way my lungs are desperate to find the oxygen they
need
the way my stomach reminds me we've not eaten in days
the way my hands reach for your side of my bed
the way my fingers yearn to trace your back one last
time
the way my legs hunt for yours to intertwine
the way my toes wiggle to diffuse the bee stings

the way my brain responds **we'd be dead if we did**

there i am again, sliced open from head to toe

lingering

(we... were happy right?)

12. screaming silence

sound is simple

the horn of a car
the bustle of a crowd
the purr of my cat
the giggles of my friends
the tinnitus in my ears
the memories of you

i've never known quiet

a person sitting in the same room
hearing nothing you are saying
a blank stare, two closed eyes
my begging and pleading, echoing
abandonment happening in live time
read receipts in the form of body language

i have known silence

13. thought training

i want to be in control

it is a belief that you can control your happiness
you just have to control your thoughts
my issue is not a lack of ability to distract my brain
the thoughts themselves are dismissible
your door being their favorite loading dock

i am trying to be in control

no, it isn't an issue with dismissing a thought
it's the magnitude of what comes after
the amplification of your absence in life
simple questioning on what could've been
wondering if i even traverse yours

i need to be in control

one thought lingers an extra moment
an advanced one accompanies eagerly
long-term memory hasn't archived this data
it's all been waiting for me to use it again
i can entertain this but just for a moment

in an instant i've been reset
as soon as a lock is picked
my fate is set for the foreseeable future
i'm revisiting the black and white
i'm reviewing the gray for new shades

i am not in control

14. grating ground

my panic attacks most often happen in my room

grounding is a common method for those with anxiety
the idea is to get your mind centralized
think of what's impacting your body
what your body can sense around you
so that your mind can come back to it

how can i ground where i was uprooted

5 things i can see
a crossword puzzle *(we completed it together)*
my red hair extensions *(red was your favorite color)*
my Eevee stuffed animal *(the costume for me, the rose for you)*
the black-out curtains *(you worked the night shift)*
a hoodie from high school *(you wore my name and i wore yours)*

4 things i can touch
my bedsheets *(the place i held you)*
my Bulbasaur PopSocket *(he's in your car too)*
an old water bottle *(you made sure i always had some)*
a 3-in-1 phone charger *(so we could share)*

3 things i can hear

the air purifier *(you're allergic to animals)*
my dog dreaming *(you always teased him for it)*
my cat scratching the wall *(RJ was your favorite)*

2 things i can smell

the pillowcase *(your scent is fading)*
my chrysanthemums *(you sprayed your cologne on them)*

1 thing i can taste

toothpaste *(you helped me restart this habit)*

only i know our memories surround me

15. love letters

poetry is such a complex thing
my notes app is full of beginnings of thoughts
organized so intently, awaiting their completion
all of them falling short of greatness

the complexity of love is the same as poetry
it can take any form, shape
it can wield various amounts of power
it can organize itself and show up differently

i promised myself not all of my poems would be sad
i know how much i love the people in my life
how my cheeks can hurt from smiling
how my ears can wiggle and move
how my eyes create waterfalls
how my laughs explode

perhaps the combined complexity is too much for me

16. melancholic melodies

can you hear the chorus?
crinkles on cheeks of well lived lives
right now your heart just feels the knives

mourning reflecting a great love lost
understanding the realism of what it really cost

in the moment you can be consumed with sorrow

relatives you only visit with for a moment
they greet you with regrets and their bestowment

a final gift to the one laid to rest
kin reunited in their best dressed

there is such a beauty in sadness

stories shared from generations before
memories being recalled like folklore

sparkles in eyes brimmed with tears
giggles amongst family and peers
the music is within us

17. puzzle piece

where do i fit in

i've often felt like the odd one out
leaving the children's table too soon
not quite old enough to understand the jokes
but hesitantly laughing along anyways

i wonder if in my overwhelming need to fit in
i've managed to damage myself in the process
if myself in it's entirety doesn't fit in anywhere
maybe it is because i have been altering myself

in the search to find what is it you're looking for
you have to try on different shoes for comfort
some too big, some too small, some too narrow
did attempting to fill these spaces change my shape?

if i am a collection of every group i've joined
will the group i was meant to join even want me?
if there is something not aligning in every setting
was i just meant to be spending my time alone?

i feel more like a kid closer to thirty
than i did when i was thirteen

why am i moving backwards
does anyone have clarity

maybe i am the puzzle, not the piece

18. soul splitting

history and habits have a tendency of repeating
themselves

repetition is a common virtue of life
souls intertwine
becoming two parts of one whole
growing, aligning, shaping into one another
two become one, so that one is no longer identifiable in
singularity

parts of you are undistinguishable from parts of me

unfortunately, souls can choose incorrectly
love is complex and cuts are inevitable
unbecoming something you know
is remembering something you never learned
parts are replaced and rewired
lives are altered and adjusted

have i always preferred my tea green apple flavored?

what then is left for the future
if you allow your soul to attach easily
if a split is repeated with each match

how will you know you've reached a final destination?
what will remain of you for them?

are you deserving of a final destination? am i?

19. oblivious organs

they don't know you like i do

her doctor says she has a bad heart
they simply haven't known her from the start

she calls me on my worst days
sometimes my thoughts begin to roam
when i feel lost, she says
"you're always with me at home"

the joy in our adventures
her passion for her hobbies
her dedication to being good
spreading herself like softbutter
supporting whoever needs it most

how is it, the organ credited with all this love
is the same organ within her that is awry

*maybe the emotional heart doesn't match the physical
heart*

20. asthma attack

breathing is supposed to be a basic bodily function
the first thing we do on our own since birth
somewhere in my development
when my structures were growing into me
there was a misalignment

shortness of breathe
pounding of drums
tingles of tips
speckles of stars
tightness of cavities

every human body is externally identifiably different
theoretically this applies internally as well
some of us have outward challenges
a missing limb, overactive hormones
some of us have inward challenges
a missing rib, overactive hormones

when will we start recognizing souls

21. hopefully happy

if you were to ask me what i want to be
my answer has never waivered
i want to be happy

there is a secret in that statement
i've always felt emotions intensely
there are subtle clues everywhere
if you just give them analyzation

yes, i want to be happy
the truth is happy is scary
if i'm not looking for clues
if there isn't always two dots
meant to find each other
if i leave well enough alone
what would become of me?

it's not that i'm looking for the negative
i'd like to think i'm not a pessimistic person
the evidence usually leads me there
is it in my framework? is it a 6th sense?

is it beautiful to desperately want what i don't allow?

www.ingramcontent.com/pod-product-compliance
Lightning Source LLC
LaVergne TN
LVHW021806210726
843510LV00018B/1654